CINCO
de MAYO

LEIA TAIT

www.av2books.com

What is Cinco de Mayo?

Every year on May 5, Cinco de Mayo is celebrated across Mexico and the United States. *Cinco de Mayo* is Spanish for "the fifth of May." This holiday celebrates the victory of the Mexican army over the French at La Batalla de Puebla, or the Battle of Puebla. Mexicans and Mexican Americans began celebrating this holiday more than 100 years ago. Today, it is a symbol of their courage, strength, and unity.

On Cinco de Mayo, people find many exciting ways to celebrate being Mexican. Crowds gather in city streets to hear lively music. They join in parades and watch colorful dance shows. They eat tasty foods made just for the event. Children dress in festive costumes and perform traditional songs and dances. People decorate their homes and public buildings with bright flowers and Mexican flags.

Special Events
THROUGHOUT THE YEAR

JANUARY 1
NEW YEAR'S DAY

FEBRUARY (THIRD MONDAY)
PRESIDENTS' DAY

MARCH 17
ST. PATRICK'S DAY

SUNDAY IN MARCH OR APRIL
EASTER

 MAY 5
CINCO DE MAYO

JUNE 14
FLAG DAY

JULY 4
INDEPENDENCE DAY

AUGUST (FIRST SUNDAY)
FAMILY DAY

SEPTEMBER (FIRST MONDAY)
LABOR DAY

OCTOBER (SECOND MONDAY)
COLUMBUS DAY

NOVEMBER 11
VETERANS DAY

DECEMBER 25
CHRISTMAS DAY

Cinco de Mayo History

In 1861, Mexico owed money to many countries. President Benito Juárez needed time to pay it back. He asked the rulers of Great Britain, Spain, and France for two years to repay Mexico's debts. The rulers of Great Britain and Spain agreed. The emperor of France, Napoleon III, did not want to wait. He decided that he wanted more than just the money. He wanted to take control of all of Mexico.

Napoleon III sent his army to conquer Mexico. It was one of the strongest armies in the world. It had not lost a battle in more than 50 years. The French troops were well trained, and they had the newest equipment. General Conde de Lorencez led the French army. Napoleon III was sure France would win.

★☆ At Cinco de Mayo celebrations in Mexico City, people reenact La Batalla de Puebla.

Porfirio Díaz led the **cavalry** at the Battle of Puebla. In 1863, he was captured by the French army. He escaped. Porfirio Díaz became the president of Mexico in 1876.

The Mexican people learned of Napoleon's attack. They formed an army to fight the French. Most of the troops were farmers with no military training. They carried knives and farm tools for weapons. Local **Zapotec** and **Mestizo** Indians also came to join the battle. The two armies met near the city of Puebla on May 5, 1862.

The United States helped Mexico win the war against the French. They gave the Mexicans weapons. Some Americans even joined the Mexican army. Many states, such as Texas and California, had once belonged to Mexico. Mexicans that lived in these states still felt very close to Mexico.

Past and Present Celebrations

CINCO de MAYO celebrations began in the United States in 1967 with a group of California State University students. They wanted an occasion to celebrate Mexican history. Today, Cinco de Mayo is celebrated across the country.

FIESTA BROADWAY celebrations were first held in Los Angeles in 1989. A fiesta is a festival celebrated in Spanish speaking countries. Today, the Festival de Fiesta Broadway is the largest Cinco de Mayo celebration in the world. The celebration takes up about 24 square blocks.

MANY AMERICANS were happy when Mexico won the war and celebrated the victory. Today, Cinco de Mayo celebrations are more popular in the United States than they are in Mexico.

Important People

The Mexican army was led by General Ignacio Zaragoza. The Mexicans attacked the French army with their **cavalry**. Then, they released a stampede of cattle to trample the French soldiers. After four hours of fighting, the French army was forced to retreat. The Mexicans had won the battle.

Before the Battle of Puebla, General Zaragoza gave a speech. His words cheered the Mexican soldiers. "Your enemies are the first soldiers of the world, but you are the first sons of Mexico. They wish to seize your Fatherland, Soldiers! I read victory and faith on your foreheads. Long live independence! Long live the Fatherland!" Later, these same words gave hope to the Mexican people.

⋆⋆ General Zaragoza was born near the Presidio La Bahia, a fort in Goliad, Texas.

★★ Benito Juárez, president of Mexcio during the Battle of Puebla, has been called the "Abraham Lincoln of Mexico." This is because both had similar backgrounds and ideas. Juárez was the first American-Indian president of Mexico.

The French invasion of Mexico was the last time any place on mainland North or South America was invaded by an overseas country. Today, the site of the Battle of Puebla is a city park. There is also a museum with a display of toy soldiers showing what happened on May 5, 1862.

First-hand Account

"Cinco de Mayo marks a singular moment in Mexican history. Nearly 150 years ago, a ragtag band of soldiers and citizens, badly outnumbered and facing impossible odds, held their ground on a muddy hill to defend their nation from what was at the time the most fearsome fighting force in the world…
[On May 5th] We'll remember that America is a richer and more vibrant place thanks to the contributions of Mexican Americans."

Speech given by President Barack Obama for Cinco de Mayo 2009.

"Cinco de Mayo has come to represent a celebration of the contributions that Mexican Americans and all **Hispanics** have made to America."

Statement made by United States Congressman Joe Baca.

Cinco de Mayo Celebrations

The Battle of Puebla was a great victory for the Mexican people, but it did not end the war. Fighting went on for five more years. During that time, the Mexican people thought about Puebla. They believed that, if they had beaten the French once, they could do it again. El Cinco de Mayo, or "the fifth of May," became a symbol of Mexican strength and unity.

In 1867, their hopes came true. The French were forced to leave Mexico. Today, Cinco de Mayo is a national holiday in Mexico and the United States. Cinco de Mayo is not only celebrated by Mexican Americans. Many cultures celebrate Cinco de Mayo every year.

★★ In Mexico City, men dress in French and Mexican army clothes during Cinco de Mayo parades.

Cinco de Mayo is one of the *Fiestas Patrias*, or "**Patriotic** Festivals," in Mexican culture. These holidays are a chance for people to feel proud. They show their pride with special symbols.

Other Hispanic groups, such as Cubans and Puerto Ricans, see May 5 as a day to celebrate their cultures. Many non-Hispanic people also enjoy this holiday. It is a chance for them to have fun and learn about Mexican culture.

Some Mexicans take part in plays about the Battle of Puebla. They wear clothing or hats in the same colors as the flag of Mexico. Men and women wear traditional clothing and perform dances during Cinco de Mayo fiestas. Some Mexicans march in parades during Cinco de Mayo celebrations in Mexico City.

Celebrations Around the World

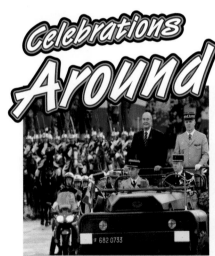

FRANCE

The end of World War II was announced on May 8, 1945. Today, people in France hold Victory Day on May 8. It is a time to celebrate freedom and the end of the war.

COLUMBIA

On August 7, Columbians celebrate the Battle of Boyaca Day. It is a day to remember the Columbian victory over the Spanish monarchy and Columbian independence from the Spanish. The battle took place in 1819.

TURKEY

In Turkey, August 30 is known as Victory Day. It is a national holiday that celebrates Turkish victory over Greek invaders in 1922. It is a day of national pride.

Celebrating Today

Cinco de Mayo is most often celebrated with a fiesta. Eating special foods, such as **gorditas**, **menudo**, and **buñuelos**, is an important part of Cinco de Mayo. Celebrating with music and dance is also part of many events. **Mariachi** bands stroll through the crowds singing Mexican folk songs. **Ballet folklórico** dancers wear colorful costumes. **Jalisco** dancers perform dances with large, circular motions. People also perform the *jarabe tapatio*, or the Mexican Hat Dance. It is the national dance of Mexico.

Many Cinco de Mayo celebrations include carnivals and fairs. People play games and buy crafts. Parades with brightly colored floats wind through the streets.

✱ A fiesta is a party. It can last one day, three days, or even a whole week. The word fiesta means "feast day" in Spanish.

The Aztec peoples founded the Mexican empire. Ancient Aztec traditions are an important part of Cinco de Mayo celebrations.

Cinco de Mayo in the United States

More than 500 cities across the United States have official Cinco de Mayo celebrations. This map shows a few of the events that take place across the country on May 5.

CALIFORNIA Los Angeles has the largest Cinco de Mayo celebration in the country. It takes up 36 city blocks, and more than 500,000 people attend. Each year, the mayor of the city gives a speech in Spanish.

California

Colorado

HAWAI'I Kona has celebrated Cinco de Mayo for more than 20 years. Mexican people have been living in Hawai'i since the 1830s. At that time, Mexican cowboys moved there from California.

Texas

Hawai'i

Alaska

0   970 Miles

0   1,278 Miles

MINNESOTA More than 100,000 visitors regularly attend St. Paul's Cinco de Mayo celebration. It takes place every year in the city's District del Sol neighborhood. Visitors enjoy a parade, dancing, music, food, and even a car show.

Minnesota

New York

COLORADO Denver's Cinco de Mayo festival began in 1987. Today, about 500,000 people attend each year. At Civic Center Park, visitors can enjoy live entertainment, a petting zoo, a chili cook off, and a children's carnival.

NEW YORK More than half of all Mexicans in New York are *poblanos*. This means that they or their parents were born in the state of Puebla, Mexico. New York celebrates Cinco de Mayo every year with a fiesta in Flushing Meadow Park. Many people attend, including the governor of the state.

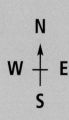

TEXAS San Marcos holds an event called the Viva! Cinco de Mayo festival every year. The festival features dancing, a pageant, a parade, and a cook-off.

N
W —|— E
S

0 _____ 207 Miles

Cinco de Mayo Symbols

Cinco de Mayo is one of the Fiestas Patrias, or "Patriotic Festivals" in Mexican culture. These holidays are a chance for people to feel proud. People show their pride with special patriotic symbols.

THE MEXICAN FLAG

Mexico's flag is made up of three bands of color. Green is on the left, white is in the middle, and red is on the right. Each color has a special meaning. The green band represents independence. The white band symbolizes religion. The red band stands for unity. At Cinco de Mayo festivals, these colors can be seen everywhere.

FIREWORKS

Most Mexican fiestas begin with the sound of *fuegos artificiales,* or fireworks, exploding in the sky. Fireworks signal that something special is about to begin. On Cinco de Mayo, fireworks light up the sky a second time after dark. Just like on the Fourth of July, they signal a happy end to a day of celebrating.

PIÑATAS

Piñatas are papier-mâché containers filled with treats. The Spanish brought piñatas to Mexico nearly 400 years ago. During a fiesta, a piñata is hung from a tree. Children are blindfolded, and they take turns trying to break the piñata with a stick. The parents move the piñata up and down with a rope. When the piñata breaks, treats spill out, and the children pick up the prizes.

A Song to Remember

Music is an important part of Cinco de Mayo. People sometimes sing Mexican folk songs. *De colores* is a traditional Mexican song. It means "All the Colors" in English. This is part of the English translation of the song.

All the colors, all the colors, oh how they dress up the countryside in springtime,
All the colors, all the colors of birdies, oh how they come back to us outside,
All the colors, all the colors in rainbows we see shining bright in the sky,
And that's why a great love of the colors makes me feel like singing so joyfully,
And that's why a great love of the colors makes me feel like singing so joyfully.

The rooster sings, he sings cock-a-doodle, doodle, doodle, doodle, doodle, doodle, doodle-doo,
The chicken clucks, she clucks, cluck, cluck, cluck, cluck, cluck, cluck, cluck, cluck, cluck, cluck, cluck, cluck,
The little chicks they cheep, they cheep, cheep, cheep, cheep, cheep, cheep, cheep, cheep, cheep, cheep, cheep, cheep, cheep, cheep,
And that's why a great love of the colors makes me feel like singing so joyfully,
And that's why a great love of the colors makes me feel like singing so joyfully.

Write Your Own Song

Songwriting is a fun way to express thoughts and ideas. Get creative, and write your own song.

Listen to a song that you like, and pay attention to the lyrics. Which words rhyme? How many verses are there? How many lines are in each verse? How many times is the chorus sung?

Start brainstorming ideas. What do you want your song to be about? Choose an event, idea, person, or feeling you would like to write about.

Write the verses. Songs usually have three or four verses. Each one will be different but should relate to the chorus.

Think of a tune for your song. Some songwriters like to write the tune before the words. Others will write them at the same time.

Write the chorus to your song. The chorus is the main idea of the song. It connects the verses together.

Many songwriters work with other people to create songs. Try working with a classmate or friend to think of a tune or words for your song.

Making a Piñata

Piñatas are used at parties and holiday celebrations. Make your own piñata. Then, break it open with friends.

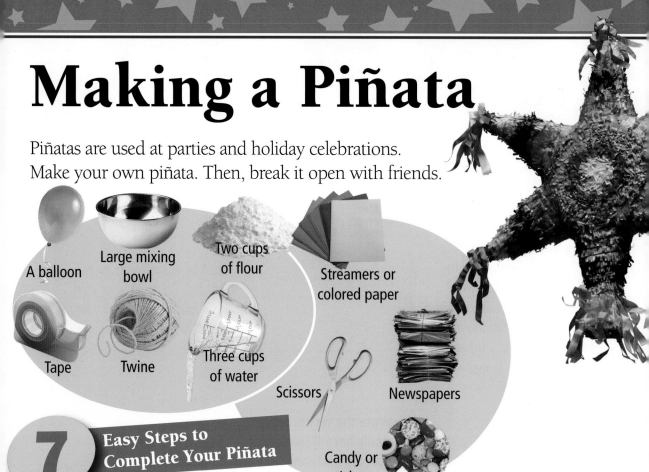

A balloon

Large mixing bowl

Two cups of flour

Streamers or colored paper

Tape

Twine

Three cups of water

Scissors

Newspapers

Candy or stickers

7 Easy Steps to Complete Your Piñata

1 Have an adult blow up a balloon and knot the end.

2 In a large mixing bowl, stir two cups of flour into three cups of water to form a paste.

3 Tear old newspapers into 1-inch-wide strips. Dip the strips into the paste, and wrap them around the balloon. Leave some of the balloon uncovered at the knotted end.

4 Allow the coating to dry completely. Once it is dry, decorate your piñata with streamers and colored paper.

5 Snip a hole in the knotted end of the balloon. Remove the broken balloon.

6 Fill the piñata with small surprises, such as candy or stickers. Stuff the hole with crumpled newspaper, and seal with tape.

7 Make a loop for hanging the piñata by attaching twine to either end of the opening. Ask an adult to help you find a safe place to hang your piñata. Then, play the piñata game with your friends.

Mexican Hot Chocolate

Ingredients

2 ounces unsweetened chocolate
2 cups milk
1 cup heavy cream
6 tablespoons sugar
1/2 teaspoon cinnamon

Equipment

saucepan
wooden spoon
cup

Directions

1. With an adult's help, melt the chocolate in a saucepan.
2. In a pot, warm milk and cream on a low heat until hot. Do not burn the liquid.
3. Add a bit of hot milk to the melted chocolate, and mix to form a paste.
4. Then, stir in the remaining milk mixture, sugar, and cinnamon.
5. Serve, and enjoy.

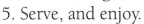

Test Your Knowledge!

1

What does Cinco de Mayo mean?

2

What is a piñata?

3

What are the colors of the Mexican flag, and what do they mean?

4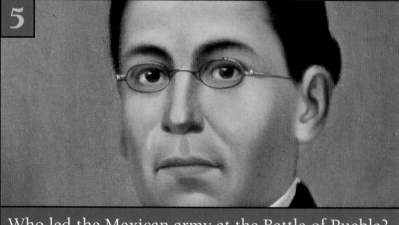

What event does Cinco de Mayo celebrate?

5

Who led the Mexican army at the Battle of Puebla?

Quiz Answers:
1. Cinco de Mayo means "fifth of May" in Spanish. This is also the day that the holiday takes place.
2. A piñata is a papier-mâché container filled with treats.
3. The colors on the Mexican flag are green, white, and red. Green stands for independence, white for religion, and red for unity.
4. Cinco de Mayo celebrates the victory of the Mexican army over the French at the Battle of Puebla.
5. General Ignacio Zaragoza led the army.

22

Glossary

ballet folklórico: Mexican folk dance

buñuelos: deep-fried pastries that are similar to doughnuts

cavalry: troops who fight on horseback

gorditas: thick tortillas stuffed with meat, vegetables, or cheese

Hispanics: Spanish speaking peoples

Jalisco: a state in Mexico

mariachi: a type of music played by a Mexican band

menudo: a spicy tripe stew

Mestizo: people who have mixed Spanish and American Indian backgrounds

patriotic: having a feeling of pride for one's country

Zapotec: American Indian group from Central America armed forces

Index

Log on to www.av2books.com

AV[2] by Weigl brings you media enhanced books that support active learning. Go to **www.av2books.com**, and enter the special code inside the front cover of this book. You will gain access to enriched and enhanced content that supplements and complements this book. Content includes video, audio, web links, quizzes, a slide show, and activities.

Audio
Listen to sections of the book read aloud.

Video
Watch informative video clips.

Web Link
Find research sites and play interactive games.

Try This!
Complete activities and hands-on experiments.

WHAT'S ONLINE?

 Try This!
Complete activities and hands-on experiments.

 Web Link
Find research sites and play interactive games.

 Video
Watch informative video clips.

EXTRA FEATURES

Pages 8-9 Write a biography about an important person

Pages 10-11 Describe the features and special events of a similar celebration around the world

Pages 14-15 Complete a mapping activity about Cinco de Mayo celebrations

Pages 16-17 Try this activity about important holiday symbols

Pages 20-21 Play an interactive activity

Pages 6-7 Find out more about the history of Cinco de Mayo

Pages 10-11 Learn more about similar celebrations around the world

Pages 16-17 Find information about important holiday symbols

Pages 18-19 Link to more information about Cinco de Mayo

Pages 20-21 Check out more holiday craft ideas

Pages 4-5 Watch a video about Cinco de Mayo

Pages 12-13 Check out a video about how people celebrate Cinco de Mayo

Audio
Hear introductory audio at the top of every page

Key Words
Study vocabulary, and play a matching word game.

Slide Show
View images and captions, and try a writing activity.

AV[2] Quiz
Take this quiz to test your knowledge

Due to the dynamic nature of the Internet, some of the URLs and activities provided as part of AV[2] by Weigl may have changed or ceased to exist. AV[2] by Weigl accepts no responsibility for any such changes. All media enhanced books are regularly monitored to update addresses and sites in a timely manner. Contact AV[2] by Weigl at 1-866-649-3445 or av2books@weigl.com with any questions, comments, or feedback.